T0329033

CAMBRIDGE LIBRARY COLLECTION

Books of enduring scholarly value

Egyptology

The large-scale scientific investigation of Egyptian antiquities by Western scholars began as an unintended consequence of Napoleon's invasion of Egypt during which, in 1799, the Rosetta Stone was discovered. The military expedition was accompanied by French scholars, whose reports prompted a wave of enthusiasm that swept across Europe and North America resulting in the Egyptian Revival style in art and architecture. Increasing numbers of tourists visited Egypt, eager to see the marvels being revealed by archaeological excavation. Writers and booksellers responded to this growing interest with publications ranging from technical site reports to tourist guidebooks and from children's histories to theories identifying the pyramids as repositories of esoteric knowledge. This series reissues a wide selection of such books. They reveal the gradual change from the 'tomb-robbing' approach of early excavators to the highly organised and systematic approach of Flinders Petrie, the 'father of Egyptology', and include early accounts of the decipherment of the hieroglyphic script.

Essay on Dr Young's and M. Champollion's Phonetic System of Hieroglyphics

Appointed Britain's consul-general in Egypt in 1815, Henry Salt (1780–1827) involved himself deeply in the excavation of several historic sites and the collection of numerous antiquities. The most notable of these, found at Thebes, was the colossal bust of Rameses II which was acquired by the British Museum and is believed to have inspired Shelley's 'Ozymandias'. This 1825 publication, featuring Salt's careful reproductions and explanations of various inscriptions, made a valuable contribution to the understanding of Egyptian hieroglyphics. Following the innovative work on the Rosetta Stone carried out by Thomas Young, and the celebrated decipherment presented in 1822 by Jean-François Champollion, Salt helped to further elucidate the hieroglyphic alphabet, although later research has disproved some of his conclusions. A postscript notes how Champollion's 1824 *Précis du système hiéroglyphique des anciens Égyptiens* (also reissued in this series) confirms several names of Egyptian gods and pharaohs which Salt had independently deciphered.

Cambridge University Press has long been a pioneer in the reissuing of out-of-print titles from its own backlist, producing digital reprints of books that are still sought after by scholars and students but could not be reprinted economically using traditional technology. The Cambridge Library Collection extends this activity to a wider range of books which are still of importance to researchers and professionals, either for the source material they contain, or as landmarks in the history of their academic discipline.

Drawing from the world-renowned collections in the Cambridge University Library and other partner libraries, and guided by the advice of experts in each subject area, Cambridge University Press is using state-of-the-art scanning machines in its own Printing House to capture the content of each book selected for inclusion. The files are processed to give a consistently clear, crisp image, and the books finished to the high quality standard for which the Press is recognised around the world. The latest print-on-demand technology ensures that the books will remain available indefinitely, and that orders for single or multiple copies can quickly be supplied.

The Cambridge Library Collection brings back to life books of enduring scholarly value (including out-of-copyright works originally issued by other publishers) across a wide range of disciplines in the humanities and social sciences and in science and technology.

Essay on Dr Young's and M. Champollion's Phonetic System of Hieroglyphics

With Some Additional Discoveries,
by which It May be Applied
to Decipher the Names of the
Ancient Kings of Egypt and Ethiopia

HENRY SALT

CAMBRIDGE
UNIVERSITY PRESS

CAMBRIDGE
UNIVERSITY PRESS

University Printing House, Cambridge, CB2 8BS, United Kingdom

Cambridge University Press is part of the University of Cambridge.
It furthers the University's mission by disseminating knowledge in the pursuit of
education, learning and research at the highest international levels of excellence.

www.cambridge.org
Information on this title: www.cambridge.org/9781108078207

© in this compilation Cambridge University Press 2015

This edition first published 1825
This digitally printed version 2015

ISBN 978-1-108-07820-7 Paperback

The original edition of this book contains a number of oversize plates
which it has not been possible to reproduce to scale in this edition.
They can be found online at www.cambridge.org/9781108078207

ON

THE PHONETIC SYSTEM

OF

HIEROGLYPHICS.

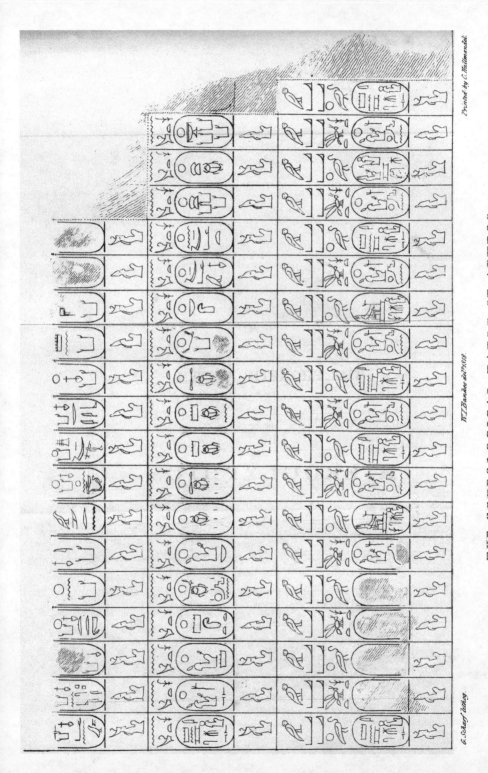

THE GENEOLOGICAL TABLE OF ABYDOS,

First discovered there in 1818, by W.I Bankes Esq: and cleared from the Sand in which it had been buried for Ages.

W.J.Bankes delⁿ 1818.

G. Scharf lithog.

Printed by C.Hullmandel.

The material originally positioned here is too large for reproduction in this reissue. A PDF can be downloaded from the web address given on page iv of this book, by clicking on 'Resources Available'.

ESSAY

ON

DR. YOUNG'S AND M. CHAMPOLLION'S

PHONETIC SYSTEM

OF

HIEROGLYPHICS;

WITH SOME ADDITIONAL DISCOVERIES, BY WHICH IT MAY
BE APPLIED TO DECIPHER THE NAMES OF THE
ANCIENT KINGS OF EGYPT AND ETHIOPIA.

By HENRY SALT, Esq., F.R.S.

HIS BRITANNIC MAJESTY'S CONSUL-GENERAL IN EGYPT,

&c. &c. &c.

ADDRESSED TO

THE RIGHT HON. CHARLES YORKE,

&c. &c. &c.

LONDON:
PRINTED BY A. J. VALPY, RED LION COURT, FLEET STREET.
SOLD BY LONGMAN, HURST, REES, ORME, BROWN, AND
GREEN, PATERNOSTER ROW.
1825.

TO THE

RIGHT HON. CHARLES YORKE.

My Dear Sir,

THE interesting Record, which forms the frontispiece of the present volume, and which is supposed to be absolutely unique, I had the good fortune first to bring to light, in an excavation undertaken for the purpose of obtaining an accurate ground-plan of the extensive ruins at Abydus. It exists there in a lesser building, quite distinct from the principal pile, which

doubtless was the Memnonium, and occupies
all that remains of a side-wall in one of the in-
nermost adyta : no portion of this side-wall
retains its original height, and it is otherwise so
much mutilated, that the table is incomplete,
both in the upper part and at one of its extremi-
ties.   The other extremity is brought close up
to the extreme angle of the chamber, and the
lowest line is carried almost down to the pave-
ment, so that in those two directions it is quite
entire.   The lithographic engraving of it here
given was executed very soon after my return to
England, with a view to immediate publication.
Some copies were distributed, and much has
been already said and written upon this table;
but the publication of it has been hitherto de-
layed; and I feel some degree of satisfaction
that its first appearance, in all its details, should
have been reserved to be thus associated with
your name, and with the ingenious labours of

our common friend, Mr. Salt; its insertion will, I trust, be received as a testimony of the sincere regard and esteem which I bear to you both,

who am very truly yours,

WM. JOHN BANKES.

1825.

Καὶ τὸ ἐν Ἀβύδῳ ἀπόρρητον δείξει.

Iamblichus de Myst.

The above sentence cited from Iamblichus (which may be translated, " and he will publish what is hidden at Abydus,") would, I have often been inclined to suspect, have no reference at all to that place if the text were properly emended, Ἀβάτῳ being the reading which I would propose to substitute for Ἀβύδῳ. Abatus was, we know, forbidden to the eyes and the feet of the profane; no such circumstance is, I believe, any where recorded of Abydus.—LONDON, 1825.

AN

E S S A Y,

&c. &c.

THE first idea of certain hieroglyphics being intended to represent sounds was suggested by Dr. Young,[1] who, from the names of Ptolemy and Berenice, had pointed out nine, which have since proved to be correct; the former taken from the Rosetta inscription, and the latter deduced with singular ingenuity from the enchorial of the same monument.[2] Working upon this basis,

---

[1] Mons. Champollion fils seems to be unwilling to allow this; but the fact is evident; and surely he has accomplished too much to stand in need of assuming to himself the merits of another.

[2] Dr. Young seems to me to stand alone with regard to the progress he has made in the enchorial, as well as for his having led the way to the true knowledge of hieroglyphics;

Mons. Champollion, with happy success, made
out four or five others, as also about thirty synonymes; and by the ingenious application of these,
the merit of which is all his own, he has been
able to turn to effect the discovery, and to decy-
pher therewith a great number of the names of
the Ptolemies and of the Roman emperors, together with their titles, which fortunately gives
us the means of determining the date of most of
the temples built within the period of their rule.

Mons. Champollion has not only accomplished this, but has suggested (though, as Dr. Young
thinks, with little success) the application of
these, or other congeneric characters, to reading
the names of the old Egyptian sovereigns,
which undoubtedly is a great desideratum, and
might lead to some important consequences in
the way of illustrating the ancient history of the
country ; at the same time that he himself states
in his " Lettre à Mons. Dacier," which is the
last work of his that I have seen on this subject,

of which, in fact, little more is yet known, than that contained in his " Vocabulary."

that "les premiers, (les noms Pharaoniques,) ca-
ractérisés par le petit nombre de leurs signes,
résistent constamment à toute tentative pour y
appliquer avec succès l'alphabet que je viens de
faire connaître."

It may be right here to state, that I had con-
ceived, from the cursory notice of this discovery
in the " Journal des Savans," and in the letters
of my friends, a very decided prejudice against
the phonetic system, as conceiving it to be
founded on too conjectural a basis ; but having
lately received Mons. Champollion's pamphlet,
as well as that of Dr. Young on hieroglyphics,
I set myself seriously to the examination of their
contents, being unwilling to suppose that so
much importance could be given, without reason,
by many persons of acknowledged talents in
Europe, to a discovery which appeared to me
only a very vague and conjectural hypothesis.
This led to a complete conviction of my error,
and induced me not only to entertain a just
appreciation of its value, from having been able
to confirm almost every point laid down by
Mons. Champollion from my own sketches, but,

with the assistance of the latter, to add some important names, as well as other phonetic characters, that are likely to conduct to results of still higher value than those already attained by its authors, and to give a new lustre to this interesting discovery.

These I shall now proceed to lay before you, and must beg your patience as I advance, it being my desire to make every step as clear and intelligible to you as to myself, which can only be done by what may appear, at first sight, too prolix an attention to detail. I must, first of all, suppose you to be perfectly acquainted with the work of Mons. Champollion; and not that you have cursorily run over it, but that you have attentively studied it, and with constant reference to the plates.

I shall now lay before you plate I, accompanying this, containing a number of rings copied entirely from my own sketches in Upper Egypt, in which you will observe that I have been able to add the names of Arsinoe and Philip the father of Alexander, and also to correct the name of Berenice. In the hierogly-

phics allotted to the last, both Dr. Young and
Mons. Champollion concur in giving a goose
of Nile as the final character; but in all the rings
that I have collected containing that name at
Karnak, Edfou, little temple near Esné,[1] Dakké,
&c., the bird is either an hawk or a crow, or
eagle, as in the name of Cleopatra; nor do I as
yet find any other bird to which the sound of
A can be attributed. Mons. Champollion, besides the goose for *A*, has given the same hieroglyphic for *Σ*, and the chicken[2] for *A*, from
his ring containing the name of Alexander; but
for neither of these do I find in my sketches
any certain authority.

The name of Arsinoe was found by me at Gau
Kibeer, at Edfou, and at Dakké—the first[3] is
clearly with Mons. Champollion's characters
APΣINE at full; the second[4] *APΣI*, with a contraction; and the third[5] *APΣN*, together with a
figure of Isis, that seems to imply goddess; and

---

[1] Vide Plate I, No. 19 to 23.

[2] I have since met with this in Signore Anastasy's name
of Necho.

[3] Plate I, No. 12.   [4] Plate I, No. 13.   [5] Plate I, No. 14.

in all three is adjoined the egg and half circle, denoting female. It is to be observed, that the one at Dakké is found in a dedication, in conjunction with the names of Ptolemy and Berenice. At Karnak, on the noble propylon there, the finest specimen of Egyptian sculpture remaining, the name of Arsinoe is found in conjunction with that of Ptolemy, who is designated as " father " of Ptolemy who had for his wife Berenice; and in the same monument is represented an image of the king Ptolemy, dressed after the Greek fashion, which is also to be observed on many other of the Ptolemaic temples.

The name of Philip[1] is still more satisfactory. It is found on the granite sanctuary at Karnak; and on the same building is repeated the name of Alexander,[2] who is termed Mi-Amun, beloved of Amun. The name is clearly expressed $\Phi\Lambda EEHO\Sigma$ in Mons. Champollion's characters, which approaches as near to the sound of the Greek as any other name discovered, excepting that of $K\Lambda EO\Pi ATPA$,[3] which accords, as it

---

[1] Plate I, No. 1.   [2] Plate I, No. 2.   [3] Plate I, No. 15.

were, letter for letter, with the Greek.¹ The

¹ The developement of an hieroglyphical alphabet is al-
lowed by Mons. Champollion to have been mainly derived
from a comparison of the several signs whose combinations
were known to compose respectively the names of Ptolemy
and of Cleopatra : he is, however, less precise in informing
us from what sources this important previous knowledge was
obtained. The name of Ptolemy had long since been published as such from the Rosetta stone, and had subsequently
been confirmed by a collation with other Egyptian monuments. The first discovery of the name Cleopatra is due
to Mr. W. J. Bankes, in 1818.

The several steps by which this name, the most perfect in
orthography of any yet decyphered, and that which has, in a
manner, furnished the key to all the rest, was first ascertained, deserve to be recorded, since, while they exhibit the pro-
cess of the discovery, they furnish also a plain and popular
proof of its authenticity.

All who are conversant with the sculptures on Egyptian
monuments will have remarked on them the multiplied re-
currence of a single figure, or of a pair of figures, offering
to the gods, or receiving something from them, in almost
every compartment, the more advanced figure, where there
are two, being the male, and the female following: in other
numerous instances the male is alone ; the occurrence of
the female singly is comparatively rare.

characters representing the name of Philip are

In each of these cases, however, it is observable that
where the pair appear once upon an edifice, they will, for the
most part, be seen similarly associated throughout; and the
same systematic repetition obtains with the figure, whether
male or female, when represented singly, to a multiplication
almost without limit, and with little other variation, excepting
in the details of the dress, or nature of the offering.

This circumstance led Mr. Bankes to suspect such figures
to have been intended rather for conventional portraits of
the founder and foundress of the building, or occupant of
the sepulchre, than for priests or priestesses, or mere mytho-
logical persons in the abstract, as more commonly supposed.
In order to try the grounds of this conjecture farther, he
caused a search to be made for the original sarcophagus in
one of the very few tombs at Thebes, (for there seem to be
only two there of any note so circumstanced,) where the
female figure is seen represented singly throughout. The
granite cover was accordingly found, and exhibits externally
a female figure, habited as Isis, sculptured in high relief;
whereas in the innumerable tombs, on whose walls the representation of the other sex predominates, this place is uniform-
ly allotted to a male with the attributes of Osiris. Thus was a
strong additional presumption obtained, that the female upon
the walls was identified with a female whose remains had occupied this depository, and the deduction seemed to extend to
other cases by analogy. Mr. Bankes next observed that, as

contained, it is to be observed, in the second

the Greek inscription upon the propylæum at Diospolis Parva furnishes the only example extant in all Egypt of the name óf a queen Cleopatra preceding (instead of following) that of a king Ptolemy, (which is to be accounted for by referring it to the regency or reign of that Cleopatra who was guardian to her son,) so does the sculpture on the same building furnish the only example, where the female figure, offering, takes a precedence over that of the man: these therefore, it seemed more than probable, must be intended for Cleopatra and Ptolemy. Accordingly, Mr. Bankes proceeded to confront the supposed name of Ptolemy, as furnished to him from the Rosetta stone by Dr. Young, with the hieroglyphical designation over the male figure, and found an exact agreement.

Here was a fresh testimony afforded to the soundness of that discovery, and the strongest presumption established, that the characters surmounting the female must be those which designated Cleopatra.

The next step was to examine, whether the same two names could be found on the shaft of the obelisk which Mr. Bankes was removing from Philæ, that being a known memorial of a Ptolemy and his two Cleopatras; and upon both being detected, not upon that only, but upon a little temple also at Philæ, where Mr. Bankes had discovered a dedicatory inscription in Greek of the same sovereigns, the matter was brought to complete proof, and the result was accordingly

ring, preceded by the goose and globe; but in
the preceding one,[1] instead of the name of Alex-

communicated by Mr. B. both to Mr. Salt and to Dr. Young,
and noted by him also in pencil in the margin of many
copies, which he afterwards distributed, of the lithographic
print of his obelisk; it was so noted, amongst others, in the
margin of that sent to Paris to be presented to the French
Institute by Mons. Denon.

To the plate of that obelisk Mons. Champollion refers
for the discovery and proof of this important name; but it
will be obvious that, without other data, a mere collation
of the Greek on the pedestal with the hieroglyphics on the
shaft could not, in this instance, have led to such a result,
the name of two distinct Cleopatras being recited in the
Greek text, whilst the only name (besides that of Ptolemy)
which occurs twice in the hieroglyphs, is not that of Cleopatra, but one which seems to contain the mystic title, whose precise interpretation is still unknown, as is that also of a fourth
name, which, like Cleopatra, occurs once only, and is different from all.

These facts are stated, not so much with a view of de-
tracting from any credit assumed, on whatever grounds, by
Mons. Champollion, as of proving that the chain of evidence
which establishes this important name is much more full
and complete than Mons. Champollion has been able to
make it appear to his readers.—LONDON, 1825.

[1] Plate I, No. 4, a.

ander, as upon Dr. Young's system might be
expected, are the images of two deities, with other
hieroglyphics, that would seem to represent
beloved (*MI*) of Amun Phre, and perhaps Osiris;
and so the name of Alexander is sculptured on
the same sanctuary,[1] in the second ring, preceded by the goose and globe, while the first
ring is filled up with his more mystic titles.

The name of Alexander is also found on the
remains of a fine ruined granite propylon on
the island of Elephantina,[2] and there too, in
the second preceded by another[3] with honorary
titles, among which is clearly to be made out the
word Amun. The name of Alexander is also
sculptured in the interior of the sanctuary at
Luxor.

The rest of plate I. will not want any other
observations than what will be found in the explanations that accompany it.

[1] The sanctuary does not appear to me to have been
erected by Alexander, as we find upon it also the name
of Rameses Thothmosis : a considerable portion of it,
however, seems to have been sculptured by his orders.

[2] Plate I, Nos. 3, 6.   [3] Plate I, No. 3, a.

I now proceed to plate II, which is entirely taken, as the first, from my own sketches, and selected from some hundred others, as representing the different names of the emperors, somewhat differently from those published by Mons. Champollion. The additions I have been able to make are the names of Nero[1] and Commodus,[2] several interesting names of Adrian[3] and Antoninus,[4] and one which appears to be Marcus Verus Antoninus Sebastos Autokrator Cæsar,[5] forming the ornaments of a cornice in the interior of a small propylon on the west of the island of Philæ. The name of Domitian alone[6] is copied from the Beneventine obelisk, as given by Zoega. From these names I have been able to deduce about twenty new synonymes, all of which are marked in the explanations of plate II, with a reference to the particular ring or rings by which they have been established, and I have noted also the temple from which each ring was taken. I have particularly to note

[1] Plate II, Nos. 5, 6, 7.   [2] Plate II, No. 22.
[3] Plate II, Nos. 14, 15, 20, 21.   [4] Plate II, Nos. 17, 18.
[5] Plate II, No. 19.   [6] Plate II, Nos. 8, 9, 10.

that the name of Autokrator Adrianus[1] is taken from the columns in the little temple near Esné, in which are inscribed two Greek inscriptions of about the same date.[2] I also cannot help referring to No. 12, as establishing clearly a character like a pair of tongs for the letter *T*, and to 14, 9, 8, as establishing the scarabee for *Δ*, *T* or *Θ*, both of these characters being of great consequence in points which I have hereafter to touch upon.

It may be here a proper place, as I am about to leave my guides, to sum up the reasons which have induced me to believe in the correctness of the phonetic system, vague as it must appear on

---

[1] Plate II, No. 20.

[2] These very interesting inscriptions, made apparently clandestinely by workmen employed in the decorative parts of this temple, were first detected and brought to light by Mr. W. J. Bankes, in 1818. They had been covered over with a thin coating of stucco, in the manner of the device recorded to have been practised by the architect of the Pharos with respect to his inscription: a very few only of the letters were discernible, till the whole was laid open by a careful scraping down of the surface.—LONDON, 1825.

the first view, and unlike as it is to every thing
appertaining to what we have been taught to
conceive of a written character. In the first
place, the fact of there being a similar usage of
phonetic characters in an existing language, the
Chinese, as very aptly instanced by Dr. Young,
is a circumstance much in its favor; then the
progress of the discovery, and the facts connected with it, the name of Ptolemy being
taken from the Rosetta inscription, and conse-
quently resting on the basis of an accompanying
Greek translation; the name of Berenice, so
happily deduced by Dr. Young from the enchorial on the same stone; the circumstance of
the same name of Ptolemy being found on so
many buildings evidently of a posterior date in
the style of their architecture to the older monuments of Egypt; the name of Cleopatra being
found as mother to a young Ptolemy at Ernent
and Koos, at the latter of which there is a
Greek inscription, in which Cleopatra is represented as reigning with her son; the same
being represented as wife to a Ptolemy at Gau
Kibeer, at Dakké, in a little temple at Philæ,

dedicated to Venus Aphrodite, and in another
discovered by me, dedicated to Esculapius, of
which I shall have hereafter to speak; in all of
which it corresponds to the same name in Greek
inscriptions found there; and also the same
name accompanying in so many other temples
the name of Ptolemy; the name of Ptolemy
with Cleopatra being, on the fine propylon at
Karnak, represented as son of Ptolemy and
Arsinoe; the name of Alexander, son of Amun,
being found together with that of Philip; the
name of Ptolemy being, as at Edfou, followed by
the title of Alexander, and by the name of Berenice his wife; the titles of Autokrator-Se-
bastos, Eusebes, Kaisar, being continually found
with the names of the emperors, but never with
those of the Ptolemies; the titles of Germanicus, Dacicus, being found annexed only to the
sovereigns who bear those titles on their medals;
the name of Adrian being prefixed, as it should
be, to the name of the emperor Trajan; the
greater part of the names of the emperors, from
Augustus to Commodus, being found on temples and edifices evidently, in their style, of a

more modern date than those of the age of the
Ptolemies, the more recent of these buildings
bearing evident marks of a very corrupt taste, as
at Contra-Latopolis, little temple near Esné, and
the temple at Kolapshi; the circumstance of
these names and titles not being confined to a
few isolated rings, but being engraved by hun-
dreds and thousands, throughout the separate
edifices, and there being no other rings in the
said edifices but what apply to those who had a
share in the construction; the ring containing
the name of Adrian being sculptured on a column, the hieroglyphics of which are known
by a Greek inscription to have been sculptured
immediately after that reign; the name of
Soter being repeatedly to be made out in
the phonetic characters among the hieroglyphics on a mummy-case of a person whose
name was Soter,[1] as appears by the inscription
in Greek written on the same case, and above all,
this name being found placed exactly after the
name of Osiris, as Dr. Young had before stated

---

[1] Plate V, No. 5.

the names of the deceased to be found in hieroglyphics on the body of most papyri.

These and many other analogous circum-
stances make out such a body of concurring
testimony as cannot in my mind be resisted,
and which the more accurately they are ex-
amined into, the more they corroborate, prove,
and establish the certainty of this phonetic
alphabet, and the truth of the deductions which
Mons. Champollion has drawn from it.

I may here premise, that it is of great consequence towards deciphering the names of the
old Egyptian kings, to which subject I shall
now proceed, to observe, that in almost all the
examples that have come before me where the
Emperors, and, in frequent instances, where the
Ptolemies are designated, the name of the king
is found in the second ring, the first ordinarily
containing their mystic or other titles, notwithstanding that the wasp and plant are placed
before the first ring, and the goose of the Nile
and globe before the last. This makes it almost
impossible, that the two latter signs[1] should re-

[1] Plate III, *d.*

present " son of," as so generally supposed, on
Dr. Young's authority, as it would render the
reading in most cases absolute nonsense; of
which I may cite as instances, the rings where
Alexander is named at Karnak, those containing the titles and name of Philip, those containing the titles and name of Cleopatra at Coos,
and elsewhere, omitting innumerable other examples that stand in the same predicament. It
struck me indeed some years ago, that the goose
and globe, the former of which, on Horus
Apollo's authority,¹ ought to represent " son,"
might rather be distinct signs, and, as we have
good reason to think that the circle represents
" Re," or the Sun, that the two together might
admit of the interpretation, " Son of the Sun ;"
and the circumstance of this very title, "ο Υιος

---

¹ Horus Apollo says, " Filium volentes significare vul-
panserem pingunt," and adds a reason for it that holds
good to this day—" that the old geese stay with their young
in the most imminent danger, at the risk of their own lives,
which I have myself frequently witnessed." " Vulpanser"
is the " goose of the Nile ;" and wherever this goose is
represented on the walls of the temples in colours, the
resemblance may be clearly traced.

Hλιου," being, in fact, placed just in the corresponding position before the name of Ptolemy in the Rosetta inscription, gives almost a certainty to my conjecture.' This conjecture is confirmed also by my having been able to trace the word " son" as designated by the goose and a single numeral, or oblong square,² denoting masculine, as in many instances at Dakké, at the little temple of Isis Thebes, on a fragment of a statue in my possession, and at Eleithias, where I first clearly ascertained the point, as also that " daughter " is expressed by the goose and a half-circle³ (the round uppermost), and likewise at Elephantina and other places.

' Since all the Ptolemies (the first only excepted) were also sons of Ptolemies, a patronymic in their case must almost always have been a mere repetition of the name; and the circumstance of the first oval differing always totally from the second on the monuments of that dynasty, is in itself enough to overturn the system of hieroglyphical patronymics as expressed in that form—a fact pointed out by Mr. Bankes to Dr. Young some years since.—LONDON, 1825.

² Plate III, *b, f, g*. ³ Plate III, *k*.

The goose and globe are also frequently
changed for a globe encircled by a serpent,
which is acknowledged to represent the Sun,
and an egg,¹ with the oblong square, as applying to a king, and the half-circle as applying to
a queen; and certainly the " egg" more naturally
represents the " goose" than, as Dr. Young
supposed, the globe and serpent. I have another circumstance to mention that will, I trust,
satisfy the most incredulous.

At Philæ I discovered, rather high up on the
side of a temple, two double inscriptions, each
in small hieroglyphical and its corresponding
enchorial characters, which seemed on examination to bear great analogy to the Rosetta inscription. Unfortunately all of them have been
cut through, and most sadly effaced by figures
and larger hieroglyphics subsequently carved on
the walls.

I made out, however, on my last journey, by
the assistance of a ladder, with great difficulty
and several days' labour, taking such moments

¹ Plate III, c.

as the sun favoured my project, a great part of
the first,' and the two last lines of one of the
inscriptions ;* and in the former we have most
fortunately the formula complete, which is
wanting in the Rosetta inscription, that runs
thus:—" Son of the Sun, Ptolemy immortal,
beloved of Pthah, God illustrious, Son of the
king Ptolemy and his sister,³ full of wisdom,
Cleopatra, God's Epiphanes;" and in the last

---

¹ Plate V, No. 1.   ² Plate V, No. 2.

³ Cleopatra could not be his sister, if the Ptolemy here
mentioned be Epiphanes, and this seemed to throw a difficulty in the way of my mode of explaining the text; but I
find since by Mons. Letronne, that this appellation was
assumed where no relationship existed. " Mais de ce ca-
ractère si décisif en apparence, on ne peut rien conclure,
depuis que j'ai établi par des preuves irrécusables que les
femmes des Ptolémées prenaient dans les monumens publics,
les titres de Sœur, " Adelphe," bien qu'elles fussent parentes
de leurs maris en tout autre dégré, ou même qu'elles
ne fussent en aucun façon leur parentes : ainsi nous avons
trouvé que ce titre de sœur fut donné à Cléopâtre femme
de Ptolémée Epiphane, et qui ne lui était parente à aucun
dégré, étant la fille d'Antiochus II. Roi de Syrie." And this
is precisely the case here. (Recherches pour servir à
l'Histoire de l'Egypte. Letronne, page 348.)

line we have, " in letters of the country, and in
letters of the priests, * * * of the first, second,
and third class; whereon is sculptured an image
of the King full of wisdom, Son of the Sun,
Ptolemy and his queen and wife Cleopatra,
God's beneficent;" [1] and, *here,* Son of the Sun

---

[1] It appears to me not unlikely, that the above decree
may be that to which the inscription on the pedestal of Mr.
Bankes's obelisk refers.

Mr. Salt, when he hazarded this conjecture, was not
aware that the Greek text of the royal decrees referred to in
the engraved inscription upon that pedestal had been discovered upon the upper member of it, and in great part
satisfactorily made out, since its arrival in England.

The letters are very little discernible, excepting by the
favour of some particular lights, having been traced upon
the plane surface of the granite in paint only, or more
probably in some oily preparation which was a ground-work
for gilding; since such a distinction might have been
thought due to this mark of royal favour: and it is perhaps
difficult upon any other supposition to account for the fact,
that these, the more important documents, are registered
upon the surface only, while the original petition is deeply
cut into the stone. The formulary of these decrees (for
there are two) has not any analogy with that deciphered by
Mr. Salt, and recited in the text. They both run in the
names of king Ptolemy and the two queens Cleopatra, the

is represented by the goose of the Nile and globe, and Son by the goose and oblong square.

There is also another circumstance which confirms my conjecture. I have a fine monument of marble, where the characters in one of the ovals (containing probably the name) have been throughout intentionally erased, and they are always those of the second ring, the characters in the first being left untouched. I have observed the same fact on several temples where the name of the founder has been displaced by that of a Ptolemy, while the titles in the first ring have been preserved as suiting equally well, no doubt, a Ptolemy as a Pharaoh.[1]

first being addressed to the priesthood, in answer to their petition, and the second a copy of their letter (requested of them in the same petition) to Lochus, governor of the Thebaid.

The former consists of seven lines; but the top being somewhat mutilated, it may possibly have extended originally to nine; the second is in eight lines. Neither of them has been yet made public, though communicated by Mr. Bankes to many friends.—LONDON, 1825.

[1] It does not seem easy to account for a singular fact first

One instance is found at Beni Hassan of the

noticed by Mr. Bankes in the temple of Luxor, and since
detected by him in many other instances, of the studied and
systematic erasure of some one particular character, where-
ever it shall have occurred as the component part of a particular name. There is a striking example of this in the
British Museum upon a sitting statue of white stone presented by Mr. Salt, where in five or six instances (that is to
say, in every instance where the rings containing names
occur on or about the figure) the first character inclosed in
the second of the two rings is purposely obliterated ; and it
makes the case the more remarkable that this is the very
same name which has undergone a similar mutilation at
Luxor, and the same which is also given in a similar state
on Mr. Salt's IVth plate, No. 13, where he mentions that
he received it from the Eastern Desert. Mr. Salt reads
the name in question Amenoph. Are we to infer then,
that in this instance the first character was not, like
all the rest, employed as a letter, but rather stood there as
some prefix of honour, or of superstition ? or, if a letter, was
there some original error or some subsequent alteration of
orthography ? The first seems the more probable solution ;
yet it may be worth remarking, that the name Amenoph
may have been sometimes written Phamenoph, as the
Egyptian month is, unless indeed the *Ph* in this case be
simply the Coptic article prefixed.

The character so carefully effaced in this instance appears

whole of the names and titles being comprised in one ring,[1] together with the wasp and plant, and goose and globe, as usually arranged. The name is that of Misarte,[2] the king who erected the obelisk now standing at Matarea. That the two rings, even of those which refer to the ancient kings, contain the name and titles of one king only, is proved from the hieroglyphics on the granite tablet below the Sphinx, where both are occupied by the name of Rameses Tothmosis, and arranged after the wasp and plant, without the intervention of the goose and globe; and it is remarkable, that the latter characters are never used throughout this tablet.

This point, therefore, I shall consider as clearly established, that the goose and globe re-

to have been a sitting male figure, resembling that of Horus. —London, 1825.

[1] Plate IV, 22. This was first communicated by Mr. Bankes to Mr. Salt, together with a parallel instance, still more remarkable, from the great Temple at Karnak.— London, 1825.

[2] The king's name is Mestres in the received text of Pliny, and Mitres in Kircher from a Vatican MS.—London, 1825.

present "Son of the Sun," and not "Son of,"
as has always hitherto been supposed.

It has long ago been remarked, and by a
very able scholar and linguist, Dr. Murray,
whose early death must long be a subject of
regret, that the names of the Egyptian kings
handed down to us are all derived from the
names of the Egyptian deities;[1] and it conse-
quently follows, that to arrive at any precise
knowledge of the mode in which these names
are written, we must become acquainted with
the signs and figures meant to represent those
deities, more especially as it seems to have
been the practice, as is evident in the rings that
contain the titles of the Ptolemies and Roman
emperors, to mix the images of the different
deities together with the hieroglyphics that represent the name.   Some idea of this kind led me,

[1] "The Pharaohs were called by the names of the Gods,
and many of the most ancient on record bear evidence of
the high antiquity of the national superstition." (Vide a
Summary View of Egyptian Mythology; Appendix to
second volume of Bruce.)

during my last voyage, to a particular study on
this point that was not unattended with success,
and this enabled me to ascertain the hieroglyphical names of several different deities that
now prove to be clearly phonetic. At the time
I was thus occupied, I confess that my patience
was nearly exhausted by observing how often
the name in a temple was varied, sometimes
being represented by hieroglyphics, sometimes
by images of the different deities, and sometimes
by the sceptre only of those particular deities;
yet, as I remarked, that there was still some kind
of order in the midst of this seeming confusion,
and that a certain manner of engraving each
name was usually predominant, I persisted in
pursuing my object, and succeeded in examining
and copying a considerable portion of the rings
with names, throughout all the different edifices
below, and at Philæ. I had before done something of the same kind, but not so much as I
could have wished, in Nubia.

At Thebes, I may observe, that I was particularly struck with the repetition of the characters and figure which I now find to represent

the Thebaic "Amun," or "Amun Re," but
which I then attributed to Phre only. In fact
it seems almost always to have formed a prefix
to the names of the Diospolitan kings.

Before I proceed to give the phonetic names
of the Egyptian gods it may not be amiss to
make you acquainted with an intermediate discovery that gave me the certainty that the
phonetic characters were in use up to, at least,
the time of Psammitichus. It had struck me
forcibly that such characters having been applied to the names of stranger kings, the Roman
emperors and Ptolemies, they would likewise,
if known, have been made use of in describing
the names of the Ethiopian sovereigns, who had
in like manner held the country in subjection
(passing over the Persian kings, which I did not
expect to meet with, from the hatred that is
known to have existed against them, as holding
the religion of the country in abhorrence); and
you may readily imagine the pleasure I expe-
rienced when I met, among my sketches made at
Abydos, with the name of ΣABAKO,[1] or ΣABA-

¹ Plate IV, No. 24.

ΚΟΦΘ, having the same termination as was found afterwards in *ΑΜΕΝΟΦΘ*. But my discovery did not stop here, or otherwise I might have had some doubts of the correctness of my application in this instance of the phonetic characters; since, soon after, I traced in a sketch taken from the back of a small portico [1] at Medinet Haboo, the name of *TIPAKA*,[2] and that so clearly expressed in characters that had now become familiar to me, as to leave no longer a doubt on the subject, the only variation being the single horizontal line for *T*, which I had not before met with, and even this difficulty being soon removed by finding the same name written with "a hand," and that from Birkel (probably Napata) in Ethiopia,[3] which M. Linant, a gentleman employed by Mr. Bankes to travel in that interesting district,[4] had kindly favoured me with; thus

---

[1] On the front of the portico the name had been everywhere erased, and the rings filled up with the name of a Ptolemy.

[2] Plate IV, 26, 27.   [3] Plate IV, 28, *a, b.* 29, *a.*

[4] M. Adolphe Linant, born at L'Orient in 1799, had been a midshipman in the French service, and visited the East in

clearly confirming the historical relation in the

company with M. Forbin and M. Prévot, whom he quitted
at Alexandria. He afterwards made the tour of Upper
Egypt and Nubia with Mr. Salt and Mr. Bankes. In 1819
he entered into an engagement to travel for Mr. Bankes,
who was then returning to Europe, but was desirous of
having his researches continued. Accordingly, in 1820,
about two months were devoted by M. Linant to a journey
into the Oasis of Ammon, and several weeks in the same
year were spent among the curious remains that exist near
Mount Sinai. The discovery of Meroë, however, was the
principal task which had been assigned to him, and in
1821 he set out for that purpose. On Feb. 22d, 1822, he
found himself among the splendid remains of that ancient
capital, which had not then been visited by M. Caillaud, or
any other European traveller. He was then on his return from
Sennaar, beyond which city he had penetrated into the
kingdom of Fasuolo so far as the 12th deg. N. lat. M.
Linant returned to Cairo in the summer of the same year. He
is now in England, and has brought over with him his very
copious notes, and a most finished collection of maps, plans,
and drawings of every thing which he saw in his several
journies.

With respect to the interesting name furnished by him
to Mr. Salt from Birkel, Mr. Bankes finds that it was
already included in his collections, he having found it upon
a detached fragment lying at a place called Shatoormeh in

book of Kings, and proving the name to be no
other than that of " Tirhakah, king of Ethiopia,
who came out to make war against Sennacherib,
king of Assyria." You may easily conceive
my delight: here was " confirmation strong as
Holy Writ," that the phonetic was in use full
seven hundred years before the commencement
of the Christian era, so far back as the time of
the prophet Isaiah, and by singular good fortune establishing the reign of a sovereign ex-
plicitly named in the Bible, yet of whose ex-
istence learned men of high literary reputation
had been pleased to doubt. I particularly
allude to Perizonius, who expresses his opinion
that Sabaco and Tirakah are one and the same

Nubia, and at Thebes, on the very diminutive propylæum of
the lesser temple at Medinet Haboo. ' It is however discernible upon the inner face only of that building, since it has
been carefully scraped out wherever it occurred upon its
outer front. On the same face where this name has dis-
appeared, that of Ptolemy has been inserted; and we thus
obtain some clue to the probable era and object of the
erasure in this particular instance.'—*This is the note made
by Mr. Bankes on the spot in* 1818 ; *agreeing exactly with
what is remarked by Mr. Salt in the text.*—LONDON, 1825.

sovereign,[1] there being little difference in the name! as also to his learned commentator,[2] who attempts to prove from Josephus that Tirakah was an Arab.

My discovery was not confined to Ethiopian kings; for, at the same moment, another name came under my eye, copied from the high granite rocks at Elephantina, and also rescued from beneath the intrusive name of a Ptolemy, from a large fallen column in front of the great temple at Karnak, and this gave in characters clear as noon-day the name of *ΠΣΑΜΙΤΙΚ*;[3] the only new character in it, which resembles a pair of tongs, having been proved to represent *T* in the name of Domitian, plate II, No. 12. The same name too is engraved on one of the small

[1] " Crediderim Sabaconem et Taracum eundem fuisse regem; rationes habeo multas; nempe, quia inter nomina Sabaconis et Taraconis exigua prorsus est differentia, &c. !"

[2] " Porro si credamus Josepho, Rex Thirhaca Arabs, non Africanus Æthiops fuit."
Herodotus agrees with Scripture History in describing him as a great Ethiopian conqueror.—LONDON, 1825.

[3] Plate IV, 30, 31.

temples at Eleithias, and, as I subsequently ascertained, on those fine monuments the obelisk Campensis and the obelisk in Monte Citorio, of which engravings are given by Zoega in his voluminous work upon obelisks.

I have here to remark, that in all the instances that have fallen under my observation, where the names of any of these kings are found, it is engraved in the second ring, the first appearing to contain a more mystical title.

I now proceed to give a short account of some of the principal Egyptian deities, and the images under which they are represented, together with their hieroglyphical as well as phonetic names, wherever I have been able to make them out; by which alone we can hope, when our information on the subject shall be more complete, to attain a knowledge of all those names which are found on the more ancient temples and are coeval with them.

I shall begin with the eight more ancient deities mentioned by Herodotus, whose names have not, to my knowledge, been hitherto exactly determined, though in my opinion they

c

can be no other than the gods Kneeph, Neith,
Pthah, Amun, Phre, Athor, Buto, and Mendes.

At the head of these we may class Knūph,
called also Ich Neuphi or Kneuph.[1] Of this
god we have the following description given
by Porphyry:—"Hujus porro Κνηφ imaginem,
humana forma depingunt, colore cœruleo, zonam
tenentem et sceptrum, pennam gerentem in
capite, ovum ab ore producit a quo nascitur
Deus quem Egypti Ptha, Græci Vulcanum
vocant."

His image as here described is not uncom-
mon in the temples of Upper Egypt;[2] and the
hieroglyphics by which he is represented are,
a chicken watching an ostrich feather,[3] or the
feather alone with a crouching figure,[4] or the flag
representing "God."[5] These are almost invariably followed by a goose and globe, or the egg
with the globe and serpent, ordinarily signifying,
"son of the Sun."

The phonetic name of Kneeph is uncertain.

[1] Plate III, A.   [2] Plate III, A. 4.
[3] Plate III, A. No. 1.   [4] Plate III, A. No. 2.
[5] Plate III, A. No. 3.

He is also the Agathodæmon represented by the image of the sacred serpent,[1] which forms the cornices of the temples and doors, is worn in front of their diadems by all the gods as well as sovereigns, is dispersed throughout their dress, holds a conspicuous place in their granaries, and is attached to every thing that was wished to be put under his protection as the " good genius."[2] He also, under this image, enters into the celebrated union of the globe, wings,[3] and serpent, placed over the entrance of all the temples in Egypt. The first is emblematic of Phre, the second of the goddesses Neith and Maut or Buto, and the last of Kneeph; by which combination it may have been intended to represent " the Sun canopied by the two firmaments,[4] and encircled by the good genius of the universe."

[1] Plate III, A. 7, 8. [2] This fact is noticed by Horus Apollo.

[3] Wings of the vulture.

[4] By the expression "two firmaments," I only refer to what was evidently the graphical mode of describing the heavens practised by the Egyptians. The two stretched-out figures are represented as one above the other in a

The second I shall describe, as appearing
in some manner to be connected with Kneeph,
is Neith,[1] one of the great goddesses representing the firmament.   Her phonetic name is
written in two different ways, with a waving
line, *N*, two feathers, *E, E,* and the upper half of
a circle, *T*,[2] or with a vase, *N*, and the upper part
of a circle, *T*, or *Θ*,[3] these hieroglyphics being
generally followed by an hieroglyphic that sig-
nifies the "firmament," which is often found
filled with stars,[4] and is occasionally changed
into one of the outstretched figures that over-
hang the zodiac.   The hieroglyphics signifying the firmament also form a sort of canopy

very interesting design on the ceiling of the great portico
at Philæ.   The lower, or that which more immediately
encircles the earth, is meant, I conceive, to represent "Maut,"
or the "Mother." The superior, Neith, which would agree
with the account given by Horus Apollo, "quoniam vide-
tur apud Ægyptios Minerva quidem superius cœli hemi-
sphærium occupasse, Juno vero inferius." The latter is evidently Maut, or Buto.

  [1] Plate III, 1, B.   [2] Plate III, 10, B.
  [3] Plate III, B, 9, 11, 13.   [4] Plate III, B, 17.

over every design of consequence throughout
Egypt. She is also represented as a human
figure with the head of a lion,[1] and as such is
the companion of Knūph; and the goose and
globe, with a feminine distinction, signifying,
"daughter of the Sun," are then generally annexed to her phonetic name.[2] On a mummy
case in my possession this goddess as an outstretched figure is represented as supported by
Knūph, who stands over a green figure recum-
bent, which may probably designate Egypt, or
the Earth.[3]

The third of the more ancient deities which I
shall notice is Pthas, or Pthah.[4] His phonetic name is described by a square, Φ, the
upper half of a circle, Θ, and a sort of twisted
cord, A.[5] These characters[6] Dr. Young has
given for "beloved;" but I feel no doubt that

[1] Plate III, 14, 15.   [2] Plate III, B, 12.

[3] Plate III, B, 16.   [4] Plate III, C.

[5] This last character changes to a small crouching figure
to the hieroglyphic representing the firmament, and the
chair which constitutes a part of the name of Isis.

[6] Plate III, C, 18.

they rather represent " Pthah," and that the
hieroglyphic or hoe which he has given for the
name of that deity designates " *MEE*," or beloved, as he himself has translated it in speaking
of one of the kings Ramesses-mee-Amun.[1]
This is confirmed also by the hoe being changed
for another character like a bier, also phonetic
for *M*, as likewise by its being often followed by
two feathers representing more exactly the sound
of *MEE*, as likewise by its being frequently connected with the names of other deities, where it
can only express " beloved," and where the name
of Pthah is wanting. Another strong circumstance in favour of the correctness of my
application of these characters (the square, half-
circle, and twisted cord) is, that in the inscription on the fine granite tablet below the sphinx
they are found incased in a square,[2] as are occasionally the names of other gods, and especially of deified kings. Pthah, according to
Horus Apollo, had for his emblem a scarabee,
and in confirmation of the correctness of this

---

[1] Appendix to the Encyclopedia, article Egypt, Section
VII. 7, and Section II. 2.   [2] Plate III, C, 26.

observation I have to remark, that in the temples
a deity is often found under the form of a
human figure with a scarabee over its head,
sometimes encircled by the globe and serpent.[1]
The great deity at Memphis, represented under
the form of a pigmy,[2] bears also a scarabee on
his head, and no doubt represents the god
Pthah,[3] as Herodotus, speaking of the derision
with which Cambyses beheld the statue of this
deity at Memphis, says, " for this statue of Vul-
can is very like those gods the Phenicians call
" Πατοικος," that they carry in front of their tri-
remes, which to those who have not seen them
I can only describe as pigmies in the "human
form." In one instance at Philæ, a deity with
the hieroglyphic of " two arms" over its head
had before it the phonetic name of Pthah,[4]
without any other hieroglyphic.

The deity I shall class as fourth is Amun,[5]
who is commonly represented by an image with

[1] Plate III, C, 24.

[2] The figures of this are very common in porcelain, and are
chiefly found in the neighbourhood of Memphis.

[3] Plate III, C, 25.   [4] Ibid.   [5] Plate III, D.

the human form, of a black colour, and the
head of a ram, surmounted with the globe and
serpent.   The hieroglyphics by which he is
designated are a chicken, or ram, watching a
vase.[1]   He is also typified by a small crouching figure with the head of a ram.   But the
Theban Jove, or Amun, is depicted as a perfect human figure, of a black colour, with a
peculiar head-dress, which is formed of the
globe and two long strait feathers.   His phonetic name is written with a feather, *A*,[2] a sort of
crown, *M*,[3] and the waving line, *N*,[4] or the eye,
an hieroglyphic like a bier, and the waving
line.[5]   It very frequently is followed by the
characters of a globe and a small oblong square,
and is then evidently Amun Phre.   It continually recurs in all Diospolitan monuments,
and forms a part of the names of almost all the
kings of that dynasty.   This image is common
in bronze.

[1] Plate III, D, 34.   [2] Plate III, D, 38, 39.

[3] This is sometimes engraved, perhaps from negligence,
without the spikes.

[4] Plate III, D, 30.   [5] Plate III, D, 31.

I shall class as fifth the god Phre,[1] or as it may have been expressed, Ph're, "the Sun," though I entertain some doubt whether he was not the second, at least, of this higher order of Egyptian deities. He is generally represented by a globe,[2] which is often encircled by the serpent,[3] and is hieroglyphically designated by the same emblem, together with a small upright oblong square,[4] which together may perhaps express phonetically Ph're. His attributes are involved in mystery, and it seems doubtful whether he was ever represented under the semblance of any terrestrial figure, unless it be that of the hawk,[5] (assumed also as their emblem by minor deities,) since it will be observed that in the rings containing the names of the more ancient kings, the globe is often changed for a small crouching figure with the hawk's head,[6] surmounted by the globe and serpent.

The next I have to notice is Athor.[7] This

---

[1] Plate III, E.   [2] Plate III, E, 42.

[3] Plate III, E, 41.   [4] Plate III, E, 40.

[5] Plate III, E, 45.   [6] Plate III, E, 43.

[7] Plate III, F.

goddess is represented under the form of a female with a peculiar head-dress,[1] composed of a globe, embraced by two upright slender horns, and surmounted by two long feathers. She is also the mystical goddess depictured by the sacred image of a cow,[2] found at the end of most papyri, and in the more secret adyta of the tombs. Her true hieroglyphical designation is the figure of a hawk enclosed in a square, with a smaller square at one of its corners.[3] Her phonetic name, which is frequently met with, is written with a feather, A, the upper half of a circle, Θ, and two convex lines meeting at each end, P,[4] with two dots under the last hieroglyphics, which usually give a double force to the character. In one instance I have found it delineated by a feather, A, two horizontal lines, (perhaps Δ, Θ) and the two convex lines, P.[5] It may be here observed that the sacred eye so frequently met with on amulets, with the appen-

---

[1] Plate III, F, 48.   [2] Plate III, F, 50.

[3] Plate III, F, 47.   [4] Plate III, F, 46.

[5] Plate III, F, 52.

dage which Dr. Young has mistaken for a tear, and the tendril issuing from it, is the eye with which Athor, when in the form of a cow, is invariably represented.

I shall class as the seventh of the greater deities the goddess Buto, or Maut.[1] She represents the lower firmament, and is designated like Neith by an outstretched female figure, which is also occasionally found as her characteristic hieroglyphic.[2] Her phonetic name is written with an upright line surmounted by a sort of Greek " Mu," M, and the upper half of a sphere,[3] followed by an egg. She is also delineated under the form of a human figure with a lion's head, and is designated as "mother," one of her titles, by the hieroglyphic of a vulture.[4] It is to be observed, that notwithstanding these two goddesses, Maut and Neith, are designated by the "vulture," yet the same emblem is assumed by other goddesses of inferior rank, a circumstance particularly noticed by Horus

[1] Plate III, G. [2] Plate III, G, 55.
[3] Plate III, G, 54. [4] Plate III, G, 56.

Apollo,[1] and that its wings are extended over their heads as well as over those of royal females as an ornament, its head being advanced before the forehead, as, in other cases, that of the agathodæmon, or snake.

The eighth and last of the great deities is Mendes,[2] or the generative power of nature. He is represented under the form of a human figure, with the head of a goat advanced in front of the forehead,[3] and designated hieroglyphically by a square, a dot, and a chicken watching over them.[4] He is represented under other forms in his generative capacity, which it will not be necessary for me here to enter upon. I have not yet discovered his phonetic name.

[1] Having so often quoted this author, I may here state, that though I am convinced, for numerous reasons, that the first book, and the first part of the second, are written by a person perfectly acquainted with Egyptian hieroglyphics, yet so am I perfectly persuaded that the remainder is a vile interpolation, excepting perhaps the three or four last hieroglyphics, which seem to have been reserved from the original work, and placed at the end, more effectually to deceive the reader.

[2] H, Plate III.   [3] Plate III, H, 58.   [4] Plate III, H, 57.

I have now to notice a few of the minor deities, and to point out their phonetic names, as well as the pure hieroglyphics by which they are designated; the latter are in general those given by Dr. Young,[1] which have since been confirmed by my own observations.

Ermes.[2]—His phonetic name is written with a half-circle turning down, and a small circle in its centre E,P, three branches of the date fruit, M, and the character resembling a pot-hook, Σ.[3] This name I ascertained at Eleithias, where different guests are marked " writer of Ermes," " priest of Ermes," " attendant of Hermes," &c. as there are others designated " writer, priest," &c. of Amun and other deities. The celestial Ermes, to which this I conceive applies, is represented as a mummy-figure with the human head, as I am led to believe, among what are termed the four Saviour Gods.

Taut or Thoth[4] is represented as a human

---

[1] The hieroglyphical designation of Amun and Phre are also from the same authority.

[2] Plate III, 1.　　[3] Plate III, I, 59.　　[4] Plate III, K.

figure, with an Ibis head,[1] and is designated in pure hieroglyphics by the same bird standing on a sort of perch.[2] This is generally accompanied by the phonetic name, two parallel horizontal lines, T,T or Θ,Θ,[3] or by a half-circle, T, or Θ, with two dashes under it, which express that it is to be doubled.[4]

Osiris.[5] His figures and emblems are well known. He is designated by an eye and a chair; as is Isis by the chair, a half-circle, and an egg;[6] and the figure supposed to be Nephthe by a half-circle or cup, the round part downwards, on a sort of square pedestal, and the two last characters as those of Isis. At Philæ is the figure of a female deity, with a crown of feathers on her head,[7] which from the phonetic character accompanying it would appear to be that of Nephthe. They are composed of an arm,

[1] Plate III, K, 63.   [2] Plate III, K, 62.
[3] Plate III, K, 60.   [4] Plate III, K, 61.
[5] Plate III, L.   [6] Plate III, M.
[7] In a Greek votive Inscription copied by Mr. Bankes, in the temple near Esneh, the goddess Nepthe seems to be referred to under the title $A\theta\eta\nu\alpha$.—London, 1825.

A, a waving line, *N*, a square, *Φ*, a half-circle, *Θ*, and a crouching figure, *E*, which may be deciphered " *ANEΦΘE.*"[1] Horus is designated by a hawk, or the figure of a child with one hand pointing to the lips.[2] The figures of these deities are so common, that it is needless for me to dwell upon them.

Anubis,[3] or the deity with the head of a fox, (commonly mistaken for a dog's,) is designated in pure hieroglyphics by a figure of the same animal. His phonetic name is very frequently found clearly expressed by a feather, *A*, the waving line, *N*, and a square, *Φ*, and in two instances[4] on a mummy case in my possession, he is called " son of Isis," which seemed to me to

---

[1] Plate III, N.

[2] Plate III, O. Horus and Harpocrates are the same. Pliny, in his chapter on the purposes to which gold is applied, tells us that "jam vero etiam Harpocratem, statuasque Ægyptiorum numinum in digitis viri quoque portare incipiunt." Some of the diminutive golden images here referred to have been found. Mr. Bankes has one of Horus for Harpocrates in his collection.—LONDON, 1825.

[3] Plate III, P.   [4] Plate III, P, 73, 74.

offer a difficulty, as being born of Nephthe, until
I found in Plutarch, according to their very
accommodating system, that " he was also con-
sidered, in one sense, as the son of Isis."

The phonetic name of Seth or Sothis[1] is very
frequent, but it is generally found accompanying the name of Isis; so that I cannot say under
what image he was depicted. It is composed
of a star, Σ, the upper half of a circle, Θ, and an
egg, Σ; the hieroglyphic like a pot-hook, Σ, the
upper half of a circle and an egg, a star, the
upper half of a circle and an adder, and other
similar characters.

Serapi.[2] This interesting phonetic name, following what appears to be a sort of water-wheel,
was found at Edfou. It is written with a star,
Σ, a crouching figure, A, the two convex lines
meeting at each end, P, a square, Π, and an
arm, I.

The figure of the deity, or genius representing
the Nile,[3] whose Egyptian name I am unac-
quainted with, is represented by an hermaphro-

---

[1] Plate III, Q.   [2] Plate III, R.   [3] Plate III, S, 82.

dite figure of a dark colour, bearing on its head a cluster of the lotus, and is generally engaged in pouring out water from a vase. It is hieroglyphically designated by three vases,[1] of the same shape as that which the figure carries united into one. The crouching figure I have given, in plate III, of this deity[2] is taken from a very curious and interesting design at Philæ ; it is encircled by the serpent, and this above and behind is enclosed by granite rocks. The Nile seems to have been worshipped only at Hajjar-Silsili, where a king is represented presenting an offering to it under the figure above mentioned. There is also a short votive inscription in Greek on the rock adjoining, addressed to the same deity.

The last figure which I shall give is that of the Egyptian Esculapius.[3] This was first discovered by me on the façade of a small temple, which I excavated on my last voyage to Thebes, and was clearly ascertained to cor-

---

[1] This hieroglyphic is given correctly by Horus Apollo.
[2] Plate III, S, 81.   [3] Plate III, T.

respond with the Esculapius mentioned in a
Greek inscription engraved on the cornice of
the same front, a fac-simile of which is given
with explanations of Plate III. It runs thus:
" Βασιλευς Πτολεμαιος και Βασιλισσα Κλεοπατρα
Θεοι επιφανες και Πτολεμαιος ο υιος Ασκληπιωι."
The figure is every where accompanied by the
hieroglyphics of a feather, (sometimes two,) an
upright line with a sort of Greek *mu* at the
top,' a roll of papyrus, and the upper half of a
circle, with a square; which I noted therefore at
the time as designating his names, and I traced
them afterwards similarly situated in several·
of the temples where the same figure is engraved.
These hieroglyphics, it will be observed, form
phonetically the name of *IMOΥΘΦ*, (which last
character may be only an expletive termination,
as it sometimes seems to be in *AMENOΘΦ* and
ΣΑΒΑΚΟΘΦ), that I find to have been the
Egyptian name of Esculapius; and this is confirmed by a papyrus in my possession, that
contains the expression " Ασκληπιου ο εστιν Ιμου-
θου υιος Ηφαιστου." It is also interesting to ob-

' Plate III, T, 83.

serve, that the same deity is termed, in the hieroglyphics accompanying the Greek inscription on the little temple, " Son, beloved of Pthah." The hieroglyphic inscription also otherwise corresponds to the Greek, in having two rings in it containing the phonetic name of Ptolemy and Cleopatra, as dedicators of the temple to Imouth.

With the assistance of the figures and hieroglyphical designations of the different deities above noticed, I have been enabled to decipher the following names of the ancient kings, or Pharaohs of Egypt, which I offer to the consideration of my fellow labourers. I have arranged them in chronological order, and formed them into a sort of table, giving first the names of the kings as drawn chiefly from the list of Manetho, and opposite each, in Greek letters, the mode in which it is expressed in the phonetic characters.

NAMES OF KINGS.	PHONETIC CHARACTERS BY WHICH EXPRESSED.
Rameses Thothmosis . .	ΡΕΜΕΣΕΣ ΘΟΘΜΟΣΙΣ (Pl. IV, 1, 2, 3, 4, 5)
Misartes	ΜΙΣΑΡΤΕΣΝ (Plate IV, 6, 2)
Amenummee	ΑΜΥΝΜ'ΑΝΥΜΕ (Plate IV, 7, 38.)

Rameses me Amun . . . ΑΜΥΝ,ΜΕ,ΡΕΜΕΣΕΣ(Plate
                         IV, 8, 9, 10, 29 c, 28 a,
                         b. 29 a. 34)
The same when in 1st ring⎞
  before the name of ⎬ ΡΕΜΕΣΕΣ ΜΕΑΜΥΝ (Plate
  Amenoth   ⎠   IV, 13 a)
Amenoth . . . . . . ΑΜΥΝΟΘΦ (Plate IV, 11, 12,
                         13 b
Ochyras . . . . . . OKIPE (Plate IV, 17, 18)
Amenummee . . . . . ΑΜΥΝΜ'ΝΑΜΕΕ (Plate IV,
                         19, 20)
Osorchon . . . . . . ΑΜΥΝΜ'ΟΣΟΡΚΟΝ (Plate
                         IV, 21)
Sabacho' . . . . . . ΣΑΒΑΚΟΟΦ (Plate IV, 24)
Tirhaka. . . . . . . ΤΙΡΑΚΑ (Plate IV, 26, 27,
                         28, 29)
Anumere . . . . . . ΡΕΝΥΜΕΡΕ (Plate IV, 27 a)
Necho, discovered by Mr. ⎫
  Anastasy   ⎬ ΝΕΧΟ (Plate IV, 29 b)
Psammitichus. . . . . . ΠΣΑΜΙΤΙΚ (Plate IV, 30, 31)
Amasis . . . . ΡΕΜΕΣΕΣ (Plate IV, 32, 33)

[1] Here perhaps might be introduced another Ethiopian
king, spoken of in Scripture, whose name was found near
Mount Sinai, who, like Sabaco or So, has erroneously been
supposed to have been an Arabian ; but the number of his
army, the mention of his allies, the Lubims, and the route
whence he came, from the coast of the Red Sea, which the
Ethiopians of Meroë for a long time commanded,—all tend

Alek-Amun . . . . . ΑΛΕΚ,ΑΜΥΝ (Plate IV, 35)

This last may probably be a contraction of the name of Alexander. I have added the names of a few other Egyptian sovereigns that I cannot trace in any author, four of which may be deciphered—Amun Athurte[1]—Amun-meerut[2] —Remeneith[3]—Rem-merun.[4]

It may not be uninteresting here to notice the names of some Egyptian queens as expressed in phonetic characters, found in single rings that precede their respective images, engraved on the walls of the temples.

NAMES OF QUEENS.   PHONETIC CHARACTERS
                    BY WHICH EXPRESSED.

Isis si Athur . . . . . ΙΣΙΣΣ'ΑΘΥΡ (Plate IV, 47)

Remeses Athur, wife of ⎫
                          ⎬ ΡΕΜΕΣΕΣ ΑΘΥΡΡ (46)
         Amenoth[5]   ⎭

to confirm the idea of his being from Ethiopia. This king is Zerah, whose name is expressed in phonetic characters ΣΣΕΡΑ, the double sigma being apparently used for a (Z) Zeta.

[1] Plate IV, 40.   [2] Plate IV, 39.

[3] Plate IV, 36.   [4] Is mislaid.

[5] There is a princess Athurte mentioned as daughter of Amenoth in Josephus.

Tasira Merun (vide king's
name above) } ΤΑΣΙΡΑΜΕΡΥΝ (50)

Tame, wife of Ramesis in
Amur } ΤΑΜΕΣΙΡΑ (51)

Tasaate . . . . ΤΑΣΑΑΤΕ (48)

Teethothe . . . . . . ΤΕΕΘΟΘΕ (49)

Amun meethe . . . . ΑΜΥΝΜΕΕΤΕ (45)

Returning to the names of the kings, I may remark, that one of the most interesting is that of
Rameses Thothmosis, who was nearly cotempo-
rary, as the best chronologists agree, with Moses.
The fine temple of Amada in Nubia, the granite
tablet before the Sphinx, the granite sanctuary
at Karnak, a small granite propylon under the
mountain at Gournoo, the obelisk at Alexandria, and other noble remains, attest the splen-
dour of his reign ; and it is certainly curious to
observe that there is not the trace of any monument remaining throughout Egypt or Nubia of
earlier date.

The next of consequence which I consider
clearly established, are those of Rameses me
Amun,' or Amun me Ramesis, and his son

' It was probably a descendant of the family who fell at

Amenoph, called erroneously by the Romans Memnon.[1] The greater part of the older monuments existing are constructed by these two sovereigns, and the tombs at Biban 'l Moluk seemto have been exclusively possessed by their family. The period in which they reigned seems to have formed the brightest period of the Egyptian monarchy. How highly the character of Amenoph was estimated at Thebes will appear by a large quarter of the city being designated after his name, and by his having been ranked, as several inscriptions testify, among even the greater gods. It is worthy of remark, that all the temples bearing the names of these kings, as well as those of Rameses Thothmosis, carry in

the siege of Troy. The Romans were proud to assert that so great a king and hero as Amenoph had fought side by side with their progenitor *Eneas ;* but it is evident that the one who fell there could have no pretension to this distinction, if any faith is to be placed in the date of the siege of Troy, which is nearly two hundred years posterior to the reign of this sovereign.

[1] I found an inscription at Thebes expressing the veneration of some person for " Memnon," whom he calls also " Amenoth, ο Θεος των Θεων πρωτων."

their appearance most convincing proof of their antiquity, evincing a style of architecture that was at once highly finished, grand, and characteristic. The remains of Ipsambul Karnak, Medinet Haboo, and the Memnonium, are glorious examples of the perfection too which Egyptian architecture had then attained, which flourished, as far as I can trace, to the reign of Psammitichus, but which may probably have continued up to the reign of Amasis and the destructive invasion of the Persians. Among the most characteristic ornaments of these more ancient edifices are the fine battle scenes[1] portrayed on their walls, in which there is a freedom of hand, and bold-

[1] No drawing has been yet published in Europe that can give any just notion of their merit. I do not in any way mean to compare Greek and Egyptian art; but I am myself convinced that Greece first received the arts from Egypt, probably about the time of the Persian invasion, when the best of the workmen fled, or were carried from their country; and the Egyptian art had just that kind of merit which was well calculated to form a good style in the hands of men of superior talents like the Greeks, unfettered by the rammels of forms unalterably conventional.

ness of design, that give us no contemptible idea of their progress in sculpture.

I shall here conclude for the present with an opinion, that the fact being now clearly established that phonetic hieroglyphics were in use in the earlier period of the Egyptian monarchy, their application will not be found to be confined to the names of gods, kings, or places. Two demonstrative articles, " ta," "pa," masculine and feminine, " en," the sign expressing " of," and " mi," signifying " appertaining to," or "beloved," have already been discovered ; and I do not hesitate to say that, with a complete knowledge of Coptic,[1] and close application to this study in Egypt, a person might be able in no long time to decipher whole inscriptions. Every where, I conceive, the real hieroglyphics and phonetic characters will be found to be mingled together, as in the rings of the Ptolemies and Roman emperors; and this of course will require a double study, in which any great

[1] Mr. Bankes ascertained that a great portion of the language called Barábra, now spoken in Nubia, is identical with the ancient Coptic. LONDON, 1825.

progress can only be the result of extreme patience and labour. For myself, to have established beyond all doubt in the phonetic characters the names of Thothmosis, Amenoth,
Psammitichus, Sabaco, and that of Tirhakah, a
king of Ethiopia coeval with Isaiah the prophet,
and mentioned by him, is, I must own, a circumstance that consoles me at last for many hours,
I may say days, occupied in these studies ; and
may serve perhaps as a hint to future travellers,
to show that there can be rarely any thing in
the shape of an ancient record unworthy of their
attention, since, though at the moment of copying
unknown characters and mutilated inscriptions,
it seems to be a very hopeless and unpromising
undertaking, there is no knowing to what important consequences it may ultimately lead.

POSTSCRIPT.

Alexandria, 7th August, 1824.

I THINK it necessary to state that I have been almost deterred from this publication by a sight of the last work of M. Champollion *fils,* in which I find that this eminent scholar has forestalled me in a great number of my names of Egyptian gods and kings. The present essay, I have to state, was written and shown to several persons in February last, when a series of family afflictions and severe illness prevented its being fairly copied out, and the plates completed up to the present time. During this period, I think at the latter end of April, M. Champollion's Egyptian Pantheon, or at least some numbers of it were shown to me by M. Le Lorraine, to whom I had communicated the scope of this essay; and on the third of August I saw in the hands of Signor Anastasy, but have not yet read it, the first copy of M. Champollion's "Précis du Systême Hiéroglyphique des Anciens Egyptiens," (Paris, 1824,) that reached Egypt;

and I can conscientiously assert that I have not altered a single word in this essay in consequence of the sight of either of his works.

Though the publication of M. Champollion's last work is in 1824, (I do not know the month,) it is not improbable that his catalogue of kings may have been made out some time before ; so that he in all likelihood may have the honour of prior discovery, as of publication. It cannot, however, but be gratifying to him, as it has been to me, to find his ideas thus confirmed by the singular coincidence of two persons in such distant parts of the globe, without the slightest communication between them, coming by different modes of deduction to the same conclusions on so unpromising and intricate a subject ; a circumstance that seems to me to afford the surest proof of the solidity of the basis on which our premises are founded—his phonetic alphabet; the correctness of which becomes thereby, I conceive, most decisively established, and it is this in great measure which has determined me to persist in the publication.

HENRY SALT.

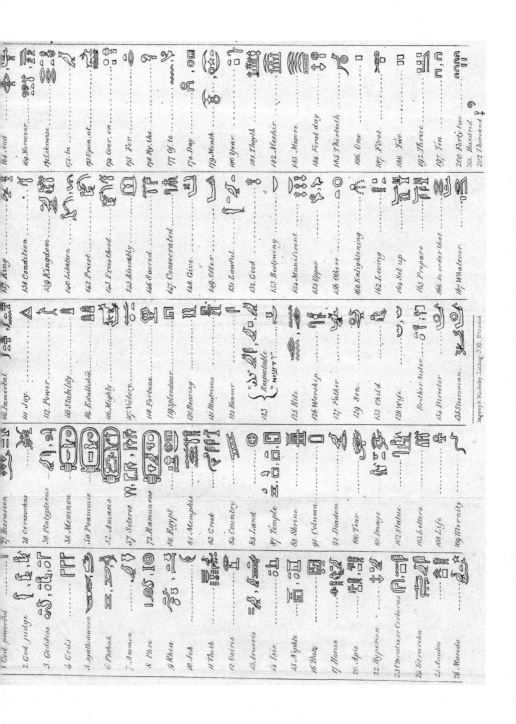

The material originally positioned here is too large for reproduction in this reissue. A PDF can be downloaded from the web address given on page iv of this book, by clicking on 'Resources Available'.

Printed by G.Vollweiler

Sadd delt.
G.Scharf lithog.

The material originally positioned here is too large for reproduction in this reissue. A PDF can be downloaded from the web address given on page iv of this book, by clicking on 'Resources Available'.

EXPLANATION OF PLATE I.

No.

1. The name of Philip (ΦΙΛΙΠΟΣ) found on the granite sanctuary at Karnak.

2. The name of Alexander (ΑΛΕΚΣΑΝΔΡΟΣ) on granite sanctuary at Karnak.

3. The name of Alexander preceded by mystic titles (*a*), in which is distinguished the word Amun, from the granite propylon on the island of Elephantina.

4. Name of Alexander, preceded by a ring (*a*), with what appears to be, " beloved of Amun Ph're."

5. Name of Ptolemy, from Philæ (ΠΤΟΛΕΜΑΙΟΣ).

6. Name of Ptolemy, from a sepulchral stone.

7. Name of Ptolemy, from Dendera.

8. Name of Ptolemy, from Philæ.

9. Name of Ptolemy Alexander, from Edfou, with the titles " immortal," " beloved of Pthah."

10. " Ptolemy," from Philæ, preceded by a mystic title, ΡΕ Κ'ΑΝΥΦ ΜΕ ΑΜΥΝ.

11. " Ptolemy," preceded by mystic title, ΜΕ ΑΜΥΝ ΦΡΕ Κ'ΑΝΥΦ, from Karnak.

12. Name of Arsinoë (ΑΡΣΙΝΟΕ), from Gau Kibeer.

13. " Arsinoë," from Edfou, (ΑΡΣΙ ⁣ ⁣).

14. Arsinoë, from Dakké, (ΑΡΣΙΝΟΕ).

15. The name of Cleopatra,from Dendera (ΚΛΕΟΠΑΤΡΑ).

16. Name of Cleopatra, from Ombos.

17. Name of Cleopatra, from Philæ.

18. Name of Cleopatra, from Medinet Haboo.

19. Name of Berenice, from Karnak (ΒΕΡΕΝΙΚΕ).

20. Name of Berenice, from Dakké.

21. Name of Berenice, from Philæ.

22. Name of Berenice, found with that of Ptolemy Alexander (No. 9) at Edfou.

23. Name of Berenice at Esné little temple.—*Mem.* The bird in this name, in twenty instances I have copied, always a hawk or eagle, and never a goose.

24. Name of Ptolemy Cæsar, found with name of Cleopatra at Edfou.

25. Name of " Ptolemy Cæsar beloved of Pthah Isis," at Dendera.

EXPLANATION OF PLATE II.

1. The word Autokrator, from a portico at Philæ.

2. Autokrator Cæsar, from a small unfinished temple, by Adrian, near Medinet Haboo, sculpture very rude.

3. Tiberius Cæsar, outside of a temple at Philæ.

4. Autokrator Tiberius Klaudius, in great temple at Dendera.

Pl. II.

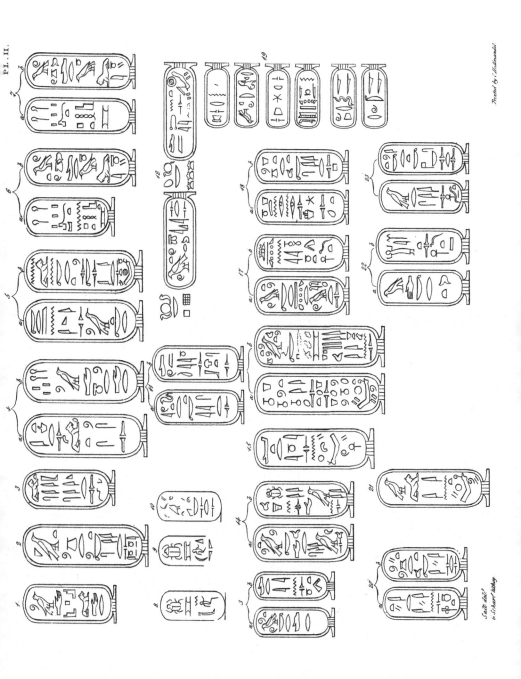

Printed by J. Netherclift

Saﬀ dd.
to Robert' Hathay

5. Neron Claudius Cæsar Germanicus Autokrator.

6. Autokrator Neron, preceded by mystic titles (*a*), side of temple, Dendera.

7. Autokrator Neron; propylon at Dendera.   Zoega has a medal with NEPΩN.

8, 9, 10. Name of Domitian, from the Beneventine obelisk, by Zoega.

11. Autokrator Cæsar Domitian Sebastos.

12. Autokrator Cæsar Domitian, from little ruined temple at Assuan.

13. Autokrator Trajan, from the Typhonium Dendera.

14. The name of Trajanus Adrian Autokrator Cæsar, from the Typhonium Dendera.

5. Name of Adrian, from little unfinished temple near Medinet Haboo.

16. Name of Antonine. The hieroglyphics at this period rudely carved and indistinct, on the first propylon at Medinet Haboo.

17. Autokrator Cæsar Antonine, from East propylon, Dendera.

18. Autokrator Cæsar Antonine Sebastos, little propylon near the water, Philæ.

19. This may be Marcus Verus Antonine Sebastos Autokrator Cæsar; it forms part of cornice round the inside of little temple near the water, Philæ.

20. Autokrator Cæsar Adrian, sculptured on a pillar with a Greek inscription, at little temple near Esné.

21. Adrian.

22. Autokrator Commodus ornaments of cornice, and last
   (*b*) over a boy at little temple of Anti-Latopolis ;
   bad work, and unfinished.

23. Autokrator Cæsar Verus, same temple as 22.

EXPLANATION OF PLATE III.

A. Figures representing the God Kneeph, and his name, in
   pure hieroglyphics.

1. Hieroglyphics by which Kneeph is designated, with the
   addition, " Son of the Sun."

2. Variation of the same, also with " Son of the Sun."

3. Another variation, also having " Son of the Sun," annexed.

4. Figure of the God, from a temple at Philæ.

5. From inside of great temple at Philæ, sitting figure of
   the same.

6. Common emblem of the same.

7. His emblem as Agathodæmon, from a drawing of a
   granary, Thebes.

8. From a mummy case.

B. Figures and hieroglyphics belonging to the Goddess
   Neith.

9. Phonetic name of Neith, with her emblematic hieroglyphic.

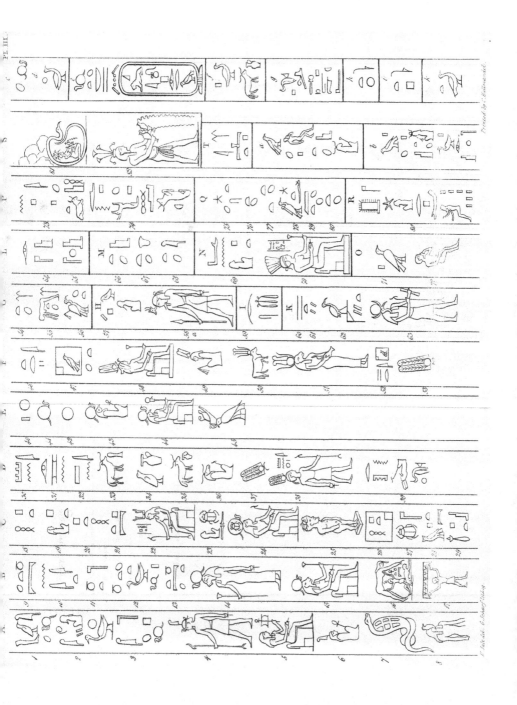

10. Another mode of writing the name, phonetically.

11. Another.

12. Another, with the addition, " Daughter of the Sun."

13. Another, with her emblematic hieroglyphic, and beneath the characters designating " female."

14. Figure of Neith, from Philæ.

15. Sitting figure of ditto, from Philæ.

16. Representation of Neith, (the hemisphere,) supported by Kneeph, the Agathodæmon, who bestrides the earth, from a mummy case in my possession.

17. A figure holding up the emblem of Neith.

C. Figures and names of Pthah.

18. Phonetic name of Pthah, very frequent.

19. Variation of the same.

20. Another way of arranging the name.

21. Another variation in the way of describing the phonetic name.

22. A figure, with the name of Pthah before it, inside of temple at Philæ.

23. His name in pure hieroglyphics.

24. The figure of the God to whom the above applies, from inside of temple at Philæ.

25. The figure of Pthah, worshipped at Memphis, frequent in porcelain.

26. His phonetic name, found on granite tablet before the Sphinx at Gheeza.

27. Another way of representing his name.

E

28. Me-Pthah, from Elephantina, or, " beloved of Pthah."

29. The same, differently expressed.

D. Figures and hieroglyphics appertaining to the God
    Amun.

30. His common phonetic name.

31. The same, differently expressed.

32. The same, without the spikes on the crown.

> These always accompany 38, generally with the addition of Ph're.

33. His pure hieroglyphic emblems.

34. Another.

35, 36. Others. These three last always accompany the
    ram-headed figure of the God.

37. Head-dress of Amun Ph're, the principal God at
    Thebes.

38. Amun Ph're, with his phonetic name.

39. Emblem of Amun, with the title, " son of the Sun."

E. Emblems and figures of Ph're.

40, 41, 42. Different ways of describing his characteristic
    emblem.

43, 44. Figures of the God, from Philæ.

45. Common emblem of the same.

F. Figures and hieroglyphics appertaining to Athor.

46. The phonetic name of the Goddess, a tablet and ring,
    at Thebes.

47. The pure hieroglyphic name of the same.

48. The figure of Athor, with her peculiar head-dress, the
    Aphrodites of Greek inscriptions in Egypt. Philæ.

49. Common emblematic figure of the Goddess.

50. The sacred cow, emblematic of Athor. Dendera.

51. A figure of ditto, from inside of a small temple near the water, eastern side. Philæ.

52. Phonetic and pure hieroglyphic name found together.

53. Head-dress of Athor.

G. Emblems of the Goddess Buto or Maut.

54. Phonetic name of the Goddess. Philæ.

55. Figure of the same, at Dendera.

57. Common emblem of the same.

H. Figure and hieroglyphical name of Mendes.

57. His hieroglyphical designation, followed by his emblematic image.

58. Image of Mendes, from three tablets in my possession.

I. The phonetic name of Hermes.

K. The figure and hieroglyphics of Thoth, or Tauth.

60, 61. Different ways of writing his phonetic name.

62. His pure hieroglyphic and phonetic names found together at Dakké.

63. Figure of Thoth, common.

L. 64, 65. Hieroglyphical names of Osiris.

M. 66, 67, 68. Names of Isis.

N. 69, 70. Figure and phonetic name of Nepthe, from Philæ.

O. Emblems of Horus.

P. Name, phonetic, of Anubis, (ANϓΦ,) styled also " Son of Isis," from a mummy case in my possession.

Q. Phonetic name and variations of Seth, or Sothis, 75, 76, 77, 78, 79, 80, always accompanying figure of Isis.

R. Phonetic name of Serapi. The figure below seems to be in the action of turning a water-wheel. The figure X is represented as such, with a figure turning it, at Edfou.

S. The God Nilus, 81, from Philæ: 82, from Hadjar-Silsili. A range of these figures is generally found on the lower basements of the temples, in the interior.

T. Figure, and hieroglyphical, or rather phonetic name of Imout, the Egyptian Esculapius, found by me, together with the following Greek inscription, on the front of a small temple which I 'excavated at Philæ:

ΒΑΣΙΛΕΥΣ ΠΤΟΛΕΜΑΙΟΣ ΚΑΙ ΒΑΣΙΛΙΣΣΑ ΚΛΕΟΠΑΤΡΑ

ΘΕΟΙ ΕΠΙΦΑΝΕΣ ΚΑΙ ΠΤΟΛΕΜΑΙΟΣ Ο ΤΙΟΣ ΑΣΚΛΗΠΙΩΙ.

a. Hieroglyphics from Dakké, expressing, "Horus Son of Isis."

b. Hieroglyphics from the same place, expressing, "Horus Son of Isis, son of Osiris.

c. Character expressing the same as (d), "Son of the Sun."[1]

d. Characters expressing, "Son of the Sun."[1]

e. Hieroglyphics expressing "Daughter of the Sun, full of wisdom, Cleopatra." Koos.

f. Characters expressing "Son of Amun," from Elephantina.

g. Characters on a monumental tablet expressing "Son of Onuphi—of Kneeph."

h. Characters that designate the Solar year.

[1] From Gau Kibeer.

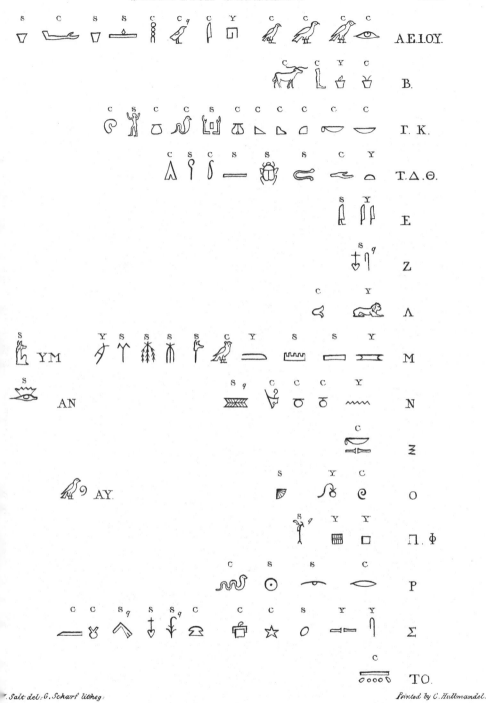

Salt del; G. Scharf lithog:

Printed by C. Hullmandel.

The material originally positioned here is too large for reproduction in this reissue. A PDF can be downloaded from the web address given on page iv of this book, by clicking on 'Resources Available'.

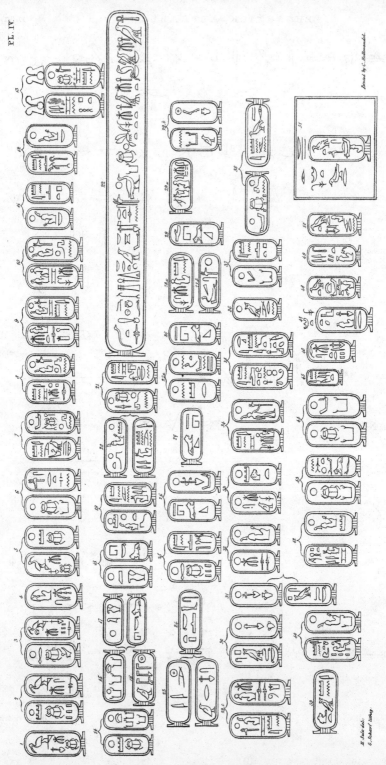

The material originally positioned here is too large for reproduction in this reissue. A PDF can be downloaded from the web address given on page iv of this book, by clicking on 'Resources Available'.

i. Characters that designate the Sothic year.

k. Hieroglyphics from a tablet where offerings are made to
    the king and queen here mentioned, Amenoth and
    Remesathorr, as Gods.

EXPLANATION OF PLATE IV.

No.
1. A ring containing the phonetic, or rather mixed hiero-
    glyphical name of Thothmosis, from Amada in
    Nubia.

2, 3. Rings containing the name of Rameses Thothmosis.
    Amada.

4. Ring with Thothmos. Amada.

5. Ring with Ramese Thothmos. Cleopatra's Needle.

6. Rings, the first of which contains a mystic title, and
    the second the name of Misartis'n, from the obelisk
    at Matarea. Pliny mentions an obelisk there,
    erected by a king of this name.

7, 38. Rings containing titles and phonetic name of
    Amunm'nummee. This is proved to be anterior to
    No. 8, by being found engraved underneath it, at
    Thebes.

8. Titles and phonetic names of Amun me Rameses, or,
    as he is styled in No. 13, Rameses me Amun. Kar-
    nak, Medinet Haboo, &c.

9, 10, 29 *a.* 28 *a.* 29 *b.* 34. Variations of the same name.
    Memnonium, &c.

11, 12, 25. Titles and name of Amenoth'ph. Colossal
   statue at Thebes.

13. Phonetic name of Amenoph, preceded by that of his
   father Rameses me Amun, found by Mr. Burton
   in the Eastern Desert.

14, 15, 16. Titles of a king, found near Mount Sinai, iron
   mines. One might suppose 16 to be that of Sesostris,
   who, we know, first conquered these mountaineers.

17. Title and phonetic name of Ochyri, from Eleithias.

18. A variation of 17. This name is found also in front of
   two stone quarries near Tura, opposite the Pyramids.

19. Titles and phonetic name of Amunm'nume II, proved
   to be posterior to Rameses m' Amun, by being found
   engraved over a ring containing his name.

20. The same written horizontally, both from Thebes.

21. The title and phonetic name of Amun me Osorchon.
   Karnak.

22. Titles and name of king Misartis'n, from Beni Hassan.

23. The name of Ermee-Zerah, an Ethiopian king, found at
   the mines near Mount Sinai.

24. The name of Sabaco'thph, found at Abydos.

26, 27. The mystic title and phonetic name of Tiraka,
   an Ethiopian king, contemporary with Senacherib,
   from behind a small propylon at Medinet Haboo.

28, 29. The same, from Birkel (Napata?) in Ethiopia.

27 *a*. Titles and phonetic name of R'Anumere, on a tablet
   in my possession.

30, 31. The mystic title and phonetic name of Psamitik, fallen column in the court at Karnak, and at Eleuthias.

31 *a.* Title and phonetic name of Necho, discovered on tablets in his possession, by my friend, by whom they were kindly communicated, Signor Anastasy, Swedish Consul at Alexandria.

32, 33. Rameses, or perhaps Amasis.

35. The mystic titles and phonetic name of Alek-Amun, perhaps a contraction of Alexander, found at Debode and Dakké.

36. The name of a king called Rammerun, to which the queen's name, 50, seems to have some relation.

37. Another Amenoth.

37 *a.* The name of a king, whose name seems to be Amunathurte.

39. The name of a king Amunmerun.

42, 43, 44. Names of kings unknown.

QUEENS.

45. The phonetic name of queen Amunmeete, from Eleithias.

46. Queen Remese Athurr, from temple at Goornu, and tablet in my possession. She appears to have been the wife of Amenoth.

47. The name of queen Isissáthor, from Hajjar Silsili.

48. The name of a queen Tasaate, from Biban 'l Moluk.

49. The name of a queen Teethothe, from a tomb in a valley near Isis' small temple behind Medinet Haboo, Thebes.

50. The name of a queen Tasiramerun, from a small temple on the island of Elephantina.

51. The name of a queen Tamesira, from Hajjar Silsili.

PLATE V.

1. The first line of an inscription on a wall of Isis' temple at Philæ, which has below it a corresponding inscription in the enchorial character.

2. The two last lines of the same. *a, a, a,* are larger hieroglyphics, that have been subsequently carved : *b, b,* heads of figures, also subsequently carved over it.

3, 4. Inscriptions from a small temple of the god Imout, excavated by me, which in some degree correspond to the inscription in Greek, given under letter T, Plate III, at Philæ.

5. Three different columns of hieroglyphics copied from a painted sarcophagus now in the British Museum, which was brought from Thebes by Sir Frederick Henniker, on which is a Greek inscription as follows:

CωTHP KOPNHΛIOT ΠOΛΛIOT MHTPOC ΦIΛOTTOC APXωN ΘHBωN.

FINIS.

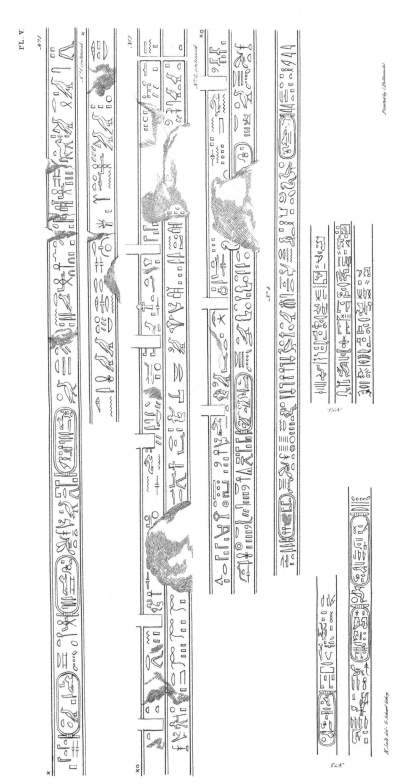

The material originally positioned here is too large for reproduction in this reissue. A PDF can be downloaded from the web address given on page iv of this book, by clicking on 'Resources Available'.